21 EASY HITS FOR UKULELE

T0039685

HAL•LEONARD®

Published by
Hal Leonard

Exclusive Distributors:
Hal Leonard
7777 West Bluemound Road
Milwaukee, WI 53213
Email: info@halleonard.com

Hal Leonard Europe Limited
42 Wigmore Street
Marylebone, London, W1U 2RY
Email: info@halleonardeurope.com

Hal Leonard Australia Pty. Ltd.
4 Lentara Court
Cheltenham, Victoria, 3192 Australia
Email: info@halleonard.com.au

Order No. AM1007413
ISBN: 978-1-78305-275-2
This book © Copyright 2014 Hal Leonard

For all works contained herein:
Unauthorized copying, arranging, adapting, recording, Internet
posting, public performance, or other distribution of the music
in this publication is an infringement of copyright.
Infringers are liable under the law.

Edited by Adrian Hopkins.
Music produced by shedwork.com

Printed in the EU.

Tuning your ukulele

The ukulele is unusual among string instruments in that the strings are not tuned in order of pitch. Watch out for this!

Here are the tuning notes for a ukulele on a piano keyboard:

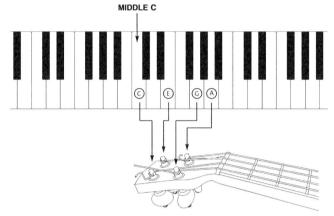

MIDDLE C

A good way to remember the notes of the ukulele's strings is this little tune:

My   dog   has   fleas!

Reading chord boxes

Chord boxes are diagrams of the ukulele neck viewed head upwards, face on as illustrated. The top horizontal line is the nut, unless a higher fret number is indicated, the others are the frets.

The vertical lines are the strings, starting from G (or 4th) on the left to A (or 1st) on the right.

The black dots indicate where to place your fingers.

Strings marked with an O are played open, not fretted. Strings marked with an X should not be played.

The curved bracket indicates a 'barre' – hold down the strings under the bracket with your first finger, using your fingers to fret the remaining notes.

N.C. = No chord.

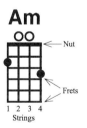

Am

Nut

Frets

1 2 3 4
Strings

G

Barre

ain't misbehavin'

Words by Andy Razaf
Music by Thomas 'Fats' Waller & Harry Brooks

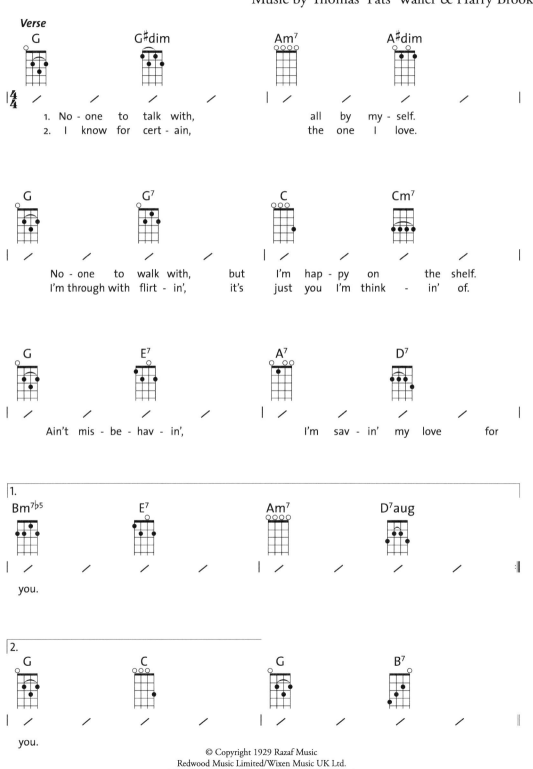

Verse

G | G#dim | Am7 | A#dim

1. No - one to talk with, all by my - self.
2. I know for cert - ain, the one I love.

G | G7 | C | Cm7

No - one to walk with, but I'm hap - py on the shelf.
I'm through with flirt - in', it's just you I'm think - in' of.

G | E7 | A7 | D7

Ain't mis - be - hav - in', I'm sav - in' my love for

1.

Bm7b5 | E7 | Am7 | D7aug

you.

2.

G | C | G | B7

you.

© Copyright 1929 Razaf Music
Redwood Music Limited/Wixen Music UK Ltd.
All Rights Reserved. International Copyright Secured.

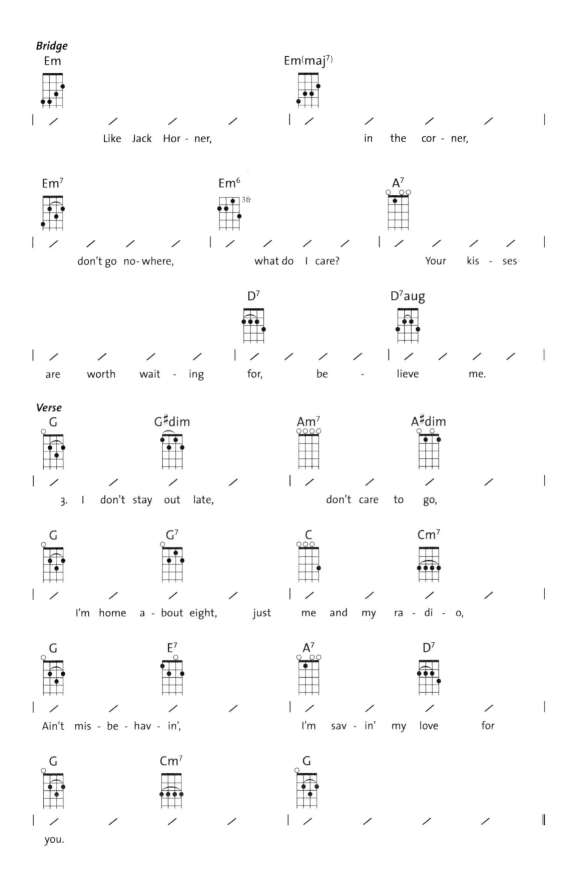

Bridge

Em — Like Jack Hor - ner, Em(maj⁷) — in the cor - ner,

Em⁷ — don't go no-where, Em⁶ — what do I care? A⁷ — Your kis - ses

— are worth wait - ing D⁷ — for, D⁷aug — be - lieve me.

Verse

G — 3. I don't stay out late, G#dim — Am⁷ — don't care to A#dim — go,

G — I'm home a - bout eight, G⁷ — just C — me and my Cm⁷ — ra - di - o,

G — Ain't mis - be - hav - in', E⁷ — A⁷ — I'm sav - in' my love D⁷ — for

G — you. Cm⁷ — G —

bird on the wire

Words & Music by Leonard Cohen

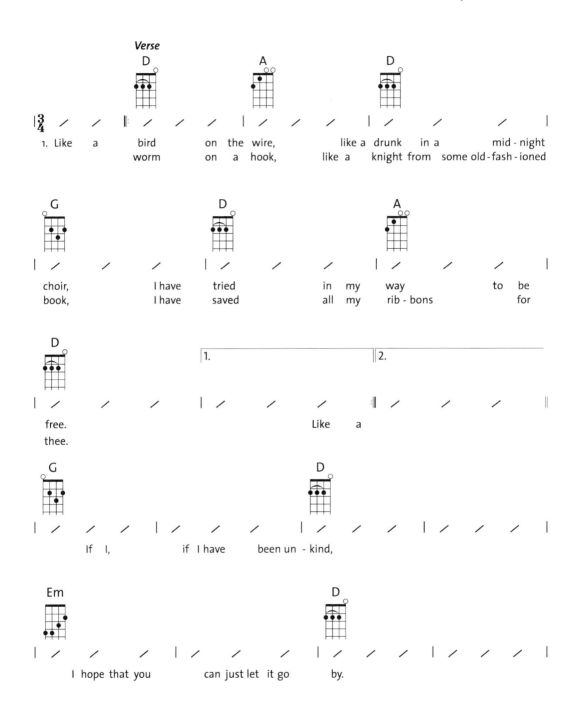

© Copyright 1968 Sony/ATV Tunes LLC.
Sony/ATV Music Publishing.
All Rights Reserved. International Copyright Secured.

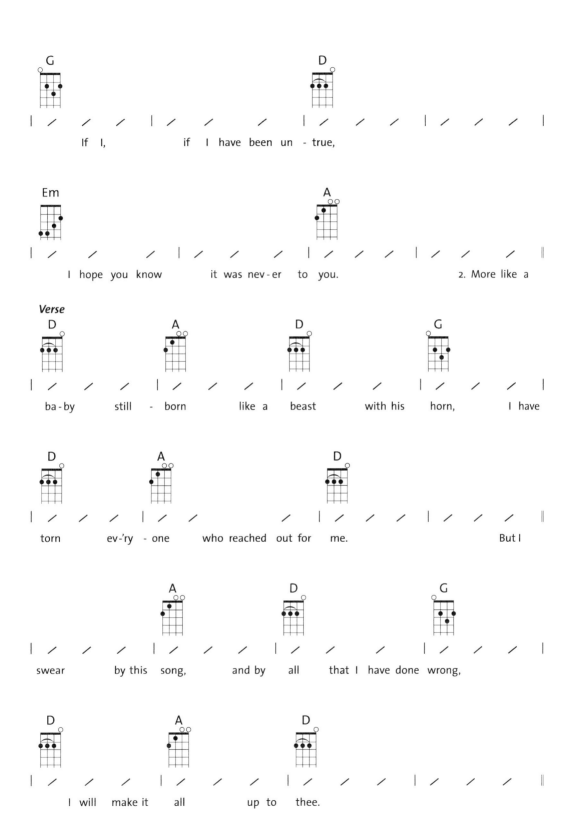

G   D

If I,   if I have been un - true,

Em   A

I hope you know   it was nev-er to you.   2. More like a

Verse

D   A   D   G

ba - by   still - born   like a   beast   with his   horn,   I have

D   A   D

torn   ev-'ry - one   who reached out for   me.   But I

A   D   G

swear   by this song,   and by   all   that I have done wrong,

D   A   D

I will   make it   all   up to   thee.

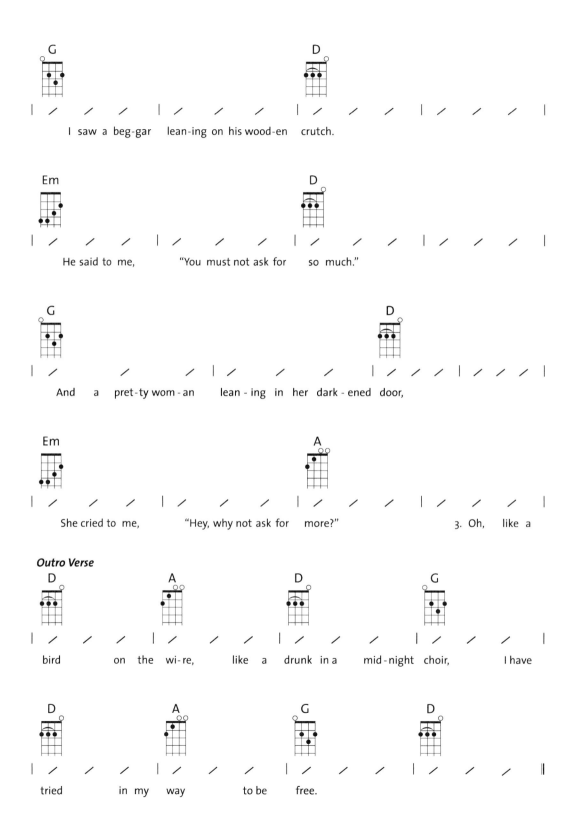

G   **D**

I saw a beg-gar lean-ing on his wood-en crutch.

Em   **D**

He said to me, "You must not ask for so much."

G   **D**

And a pret-ty wom-an lean-ing in her dark-ened door,

Em   **A**

She cried to me, "Hey, why not ask for more?" 3. Oh, like a

Outro Verse

D   **A**   **D**   **G**

bird on the wi-re, like a drunk in a mid-night choir, I have

D   **A**   **G**   **D**

tried in my way to be free.

crazy

Words & Music by Thomas Callaway, Brian Burton,
Gianfranco Reverberi & Gian Piero Reverberi

Verse

Cm

1. I re-mem-ber when,   I re - mem-ber, I re-mem-ber when I lost my   mind.

E♭maj7

There was some-thing so plea-sant a-bout that place.

A♭add9   **A♭**

Ev-en your e-mo-tions had an e - cho in so much space.

Gsus4   **G**

Cm

And when you're out there,   with-out   care,   yeah, I was out of   touch.

2. Come on now, who do   you, who do   you, who do you, who do you think you

© Copyright 2006 Chrysalis Music Limited/Warner/Chappell Music Publishing Limited/Atmosphere Music Limited.
All Rights Reserved. International Copyright Secured.

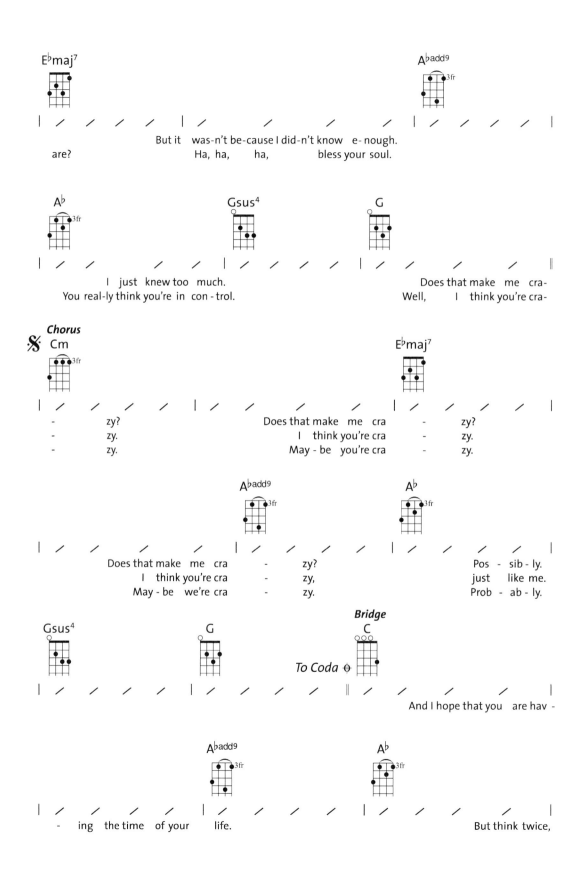

E♭maj⁷   A♭add9

But it was-n't be-cause I did-n't know e-nough.
are? Ha, ha, ha, bless your soul.

A♭   Gsus⁴   G

I just knew too much.
You real-ly think you're in con-trol.

Does that make me cra-
Well, I think you're cra-

Chorus
Cm   E♭maj⁷

-     zy?   Does that make me cra   -   zy?
-     zy.   I think you're cra   -   zy.
-     zy.   May - be you're cra   -   zy.

A♭add9   A♭

Does that make me cra   -   zy?   Pos - sib - ly.
I think you're cra   -   zy,   just like me.
May - be we're cra   -   zy.   Prob - ab - ly.

Gsus⁴   G   **Bridge**
                                                 C

To Coda ⊕

And I hope that you are hav -

A♭add9   A♭

- ing the time of your life.   But think twice,

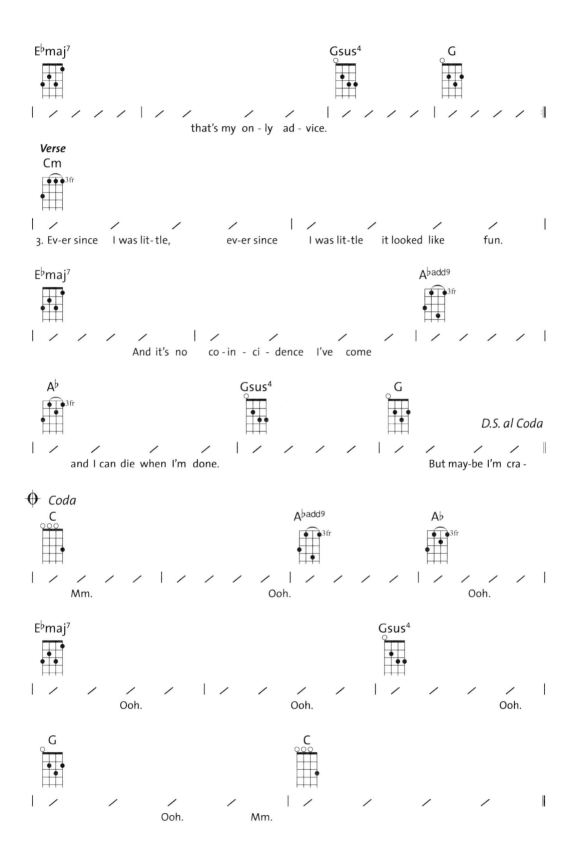

that's my on - ly ad - vice.

Verse

3. Ev-er since   I was lit-tle,   ev-er since   I was lit-tle   it looked like   fun.

And it's no   co - in - ci - dence   I've   come

D.S. al Coda

and I can die when I'm done.   But may-be I'm cra -

Coda

Mm.   Ooh.   Ooh.

Ooh.   Ooh.   Ooh.

Ooh.   Mm.

every breath you take

Words & Music by Sting

© Copyright 1983 GM Sumner.
All Rights Reserved. International Copyright Secured.

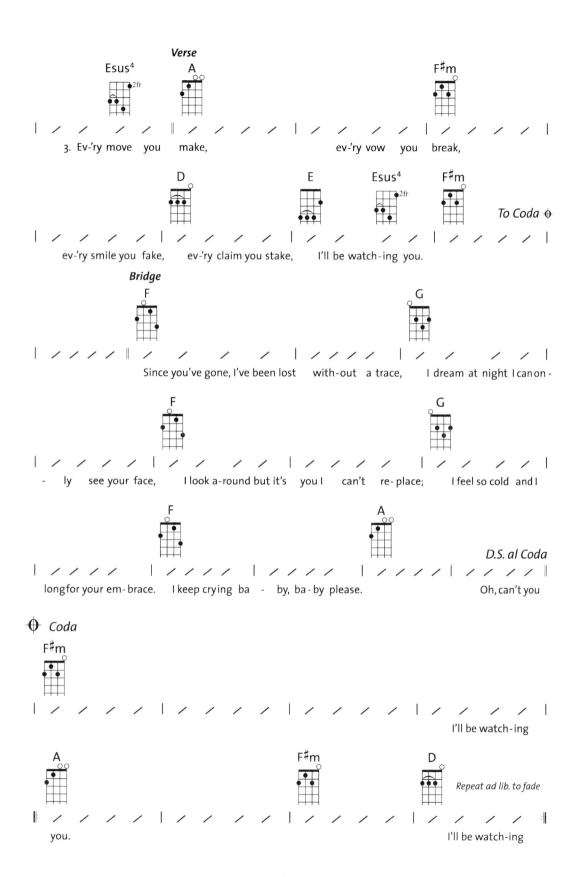

Verse

Esus⁴   A   F♯m

3. Ev-'ry move you make,   ev-'ry vow you break,

D   E   Esus⁴   F♯m

To Coda ⊕

ev-'ry smile you fake,   ev-'ry claim you stake,   I'll be watch-ing you.

Bridge

F   G

Since you've gone, I've been lost   with-out a trace,   I dream at night I can on-

F   G

- ly see your face,   I look a-round but it's you I can't re-place;   I feel so cold and I

F   A

D.S. al Coda

long for your em-brace.   I keep crying ba - by, ba-by please.   Oh, can't you

⊕ *Coda*

F♯m

I'll be watch-ing

A   F♯m   D

Repeat ad lib. to fade

you.   I'll be watch-ing

hallelujah

Words & Music by Leonard Cohen

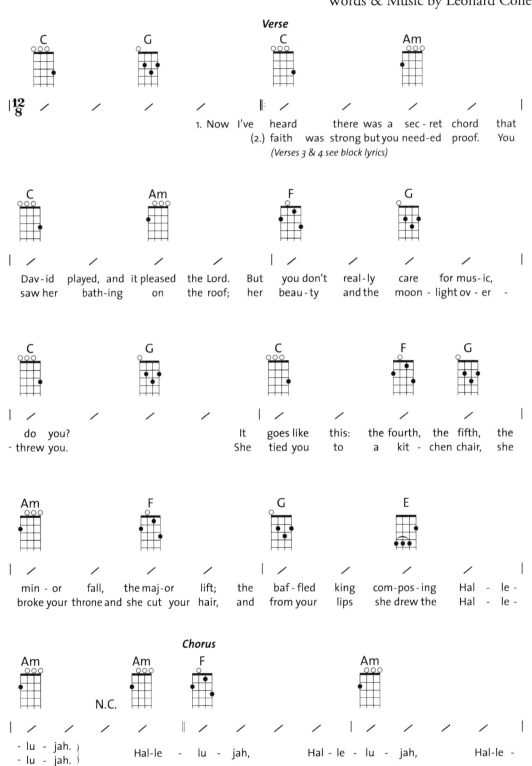

Verse

C   G   C   Am

1. Now I've heard there was a sec - ret chord that
(2.) faith was strong but you need-ed proof. You

(Verses 3 & 4 see block lyrics)

C   Am   F   G

Dav-id played, and it pleased the Lord. But you don't real-ly care for mus-ic,
saw her bath-ing on the roof; her beau-ty and the moon-light ov-er -

C   G   C   F   G

do you? It goes like this: the fourth, the fifth, the
- threw you. She tied you to a kit - chen chair, she

Am   F   G   E

min - or fall, the maj-or lift; the baf-fled king com-pos-ing Hal - le -
broke your throne and she cut your hair, and from your lips she drew the Hal - le -

Chorus

Am   N.C.   Am   F   Am

- lu - jah. }
- lu - jah. }   Hal-le - lu - jah, Hal - le - lu - jah, Hal-le -

© Copyright 1984 Bad Monk Publishing.
Sony/ATV Music Publishing.
All Rights Reserved. International Copyright Secured.

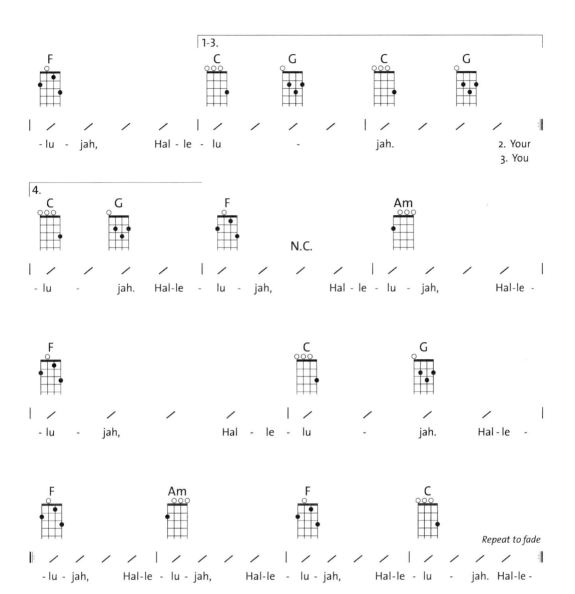

1-3.

F | C G | C G

- lu - jah, Hal - le - lu - jah.

2. Your
3. You

4.

C G | F | Am

- lu - jah. Hal-le - lu - jah,   N.C.   Hal - le - lu - jah,   Hal-le -

F | C G

- lu - jah, Hal - le - lu - jah.   Hal - le -

F | Am | F | C

Repeat to fade

- lu - jah, Hal-le - lu - jah,   Hal-le - lu - jah,   Hal-le - lu - jah. Hal-le -

Verse 3
You say I took the name in vain
I don't even know the name
But if I did, well really, what's it to you?
There's a blaze of light in every word
It doesn't matter which you heard
The holy or the broken Hallelujah.

Hallelujah *etc.*

Verse 4
I did my best, it wasn't much
I couldn't feel, so I tried to touch
I've told the truth, I didn't come to fool you.
And even though it all went wrong
I'll stand before the Lord of Song
With nothing on my tongue but Hallelujah.

Hallelujah *etc.*

help!

Words & Music by John Lennon & Paul McCartney

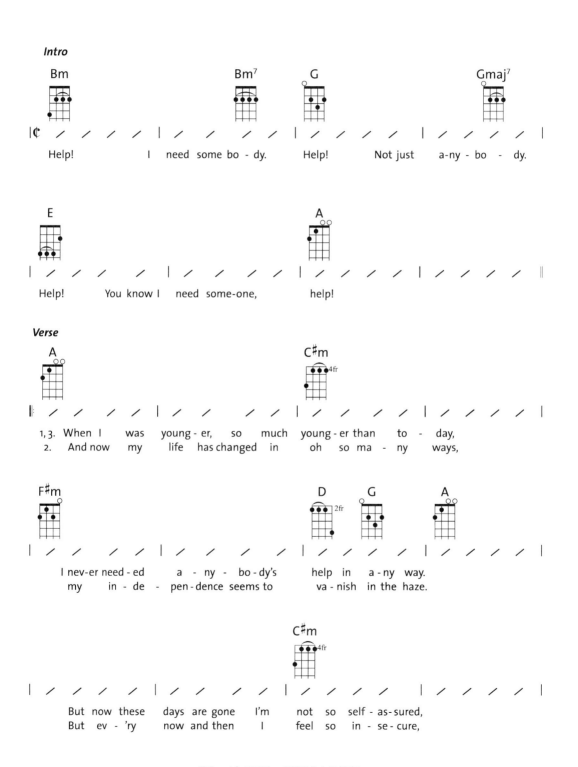

Intro

Bm   Bm⁷   G   Gmaj⁷

Help!   I need some bo - dy.   Help!   Not just a-ny-bo - dy.

E   A

Help!   You know I need some-one,   help!

Verse

A   C#m

1, 3. When I was young-er, so much young-er than to - day,
2. And now my life has changed in oh so ma-ny ways,

F#m   D   G   A

I nev-er need-ed a-ny-bo-dy's help in a-ny way.
my in-de-pen-dence seems to va-nish in the haze.

C#m

But now these days are gone I'm not so self-as-sured,
But ev-'ry now and then I feel so in-se-cure,

© Copyright 1965 Sony/ATV Music Publishing.
All Rights Reserved. International Copyright Secured.

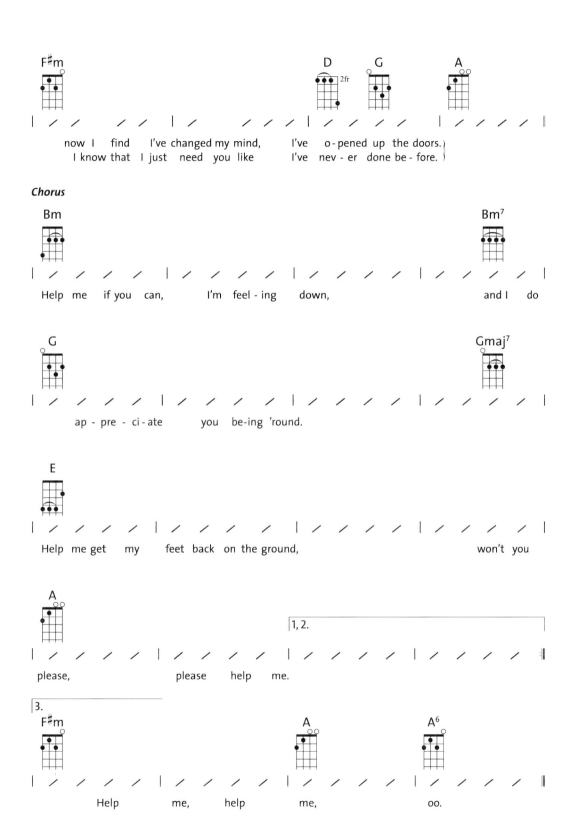

F#m   D   G   A

now I   find   I've changed my mind,   I've   o - pened up   the doors.
I know that   I just   need   you like   I've   nev - er   done be - fore.

Chorus

Bm   Bm^7

Help   me   if you   can,   I'm   feel - ing   down,   and I   do

G   Gmaj^7

ap - pre - ci - ate   you   be-ing 'round.

E

Help   me get   my   feet back   on the ground,   won't you

A

1, 2.

please,   please   help   me.

3.

F#m   A   A^6

Help   me,   help   me,   oo.

greensleeves

Traditional

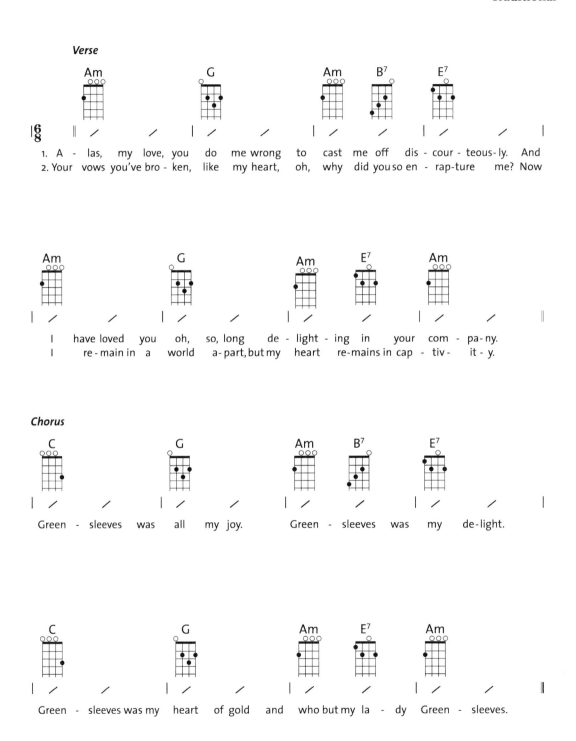

Verse

Am · · · | G · · | Am B7 · | E7 · · |

1. A - las, my love, you do me wrong to cast me off dis - cour - teous- ly. And
2. Your vows you've bro - ken, like my heart, oh, why did you so en - rap-ture me? Now

Am · · | G · · | Am E7 · | Am · · |

I have loved you oh, so, long de - light - ing in your com - pa - ny.
I re - main in a world a-part, but my heart re-mains in cap - tiv - it - y.

Chorus

C · · | G · · | Am B7 · | E7 · · |

Green - sleeves was all my joy. Green - sleeves was my de -light.

C · · | G · · | Am E7 · | Am · · |

Green - sleeves was my heart of gold and who but my la - dy Green - sleeves.

© Copyright 2013 Dorsey Brothers Music Limited.
All Rights Reserved. International Copyright Secured.

i walk the line

Words & Music by Johnny Cash

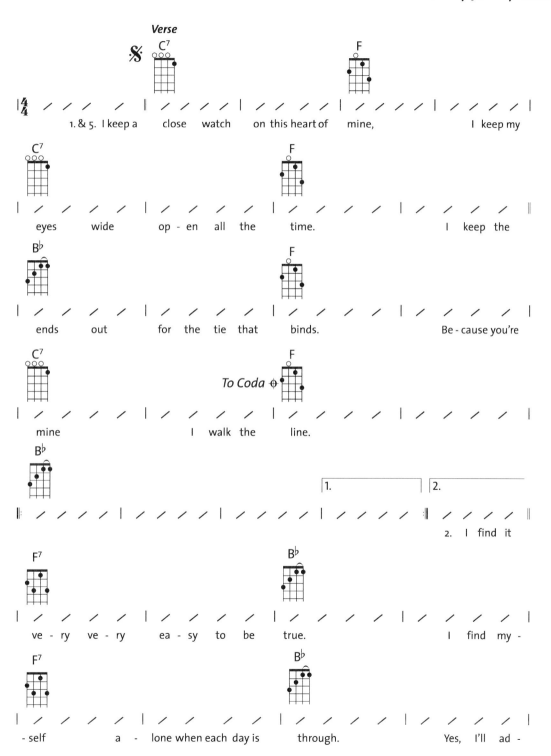

© Copyright 1956 Hill & Range Songs Incorporated.
Carlin Music Corporation.
All Rights Reserved. International Copyright Secured.

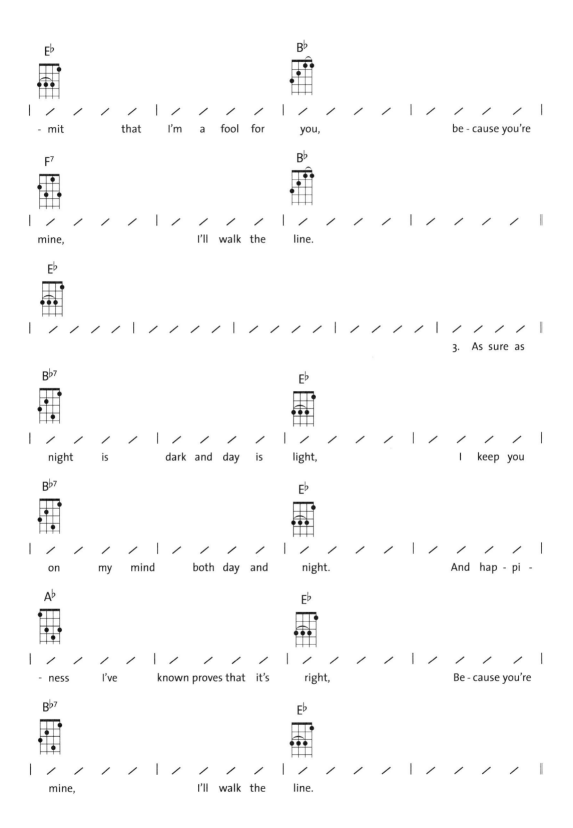

| E♭ |

/ / / / | / / / / | / / / / | / / / / |

- mit   that   I'm a fool for   you,   be - cause you're

| F⁷ | B♭ |

mine,   I'll walk the   line.

| E♭ |

3. As sure as

| B♭⁷ | E♭ |

night   is   dark and day is   light,   I   keep you

| B♭⁷ | E♭ |

on   my mind   both day and   night.   And hap - pi -

| A♭ | E♭ |

- ness   I've   known proves that it's   right,   Be - cause you're

| B♭⁷ | E♭ |

mine,   I'll walk the   line.

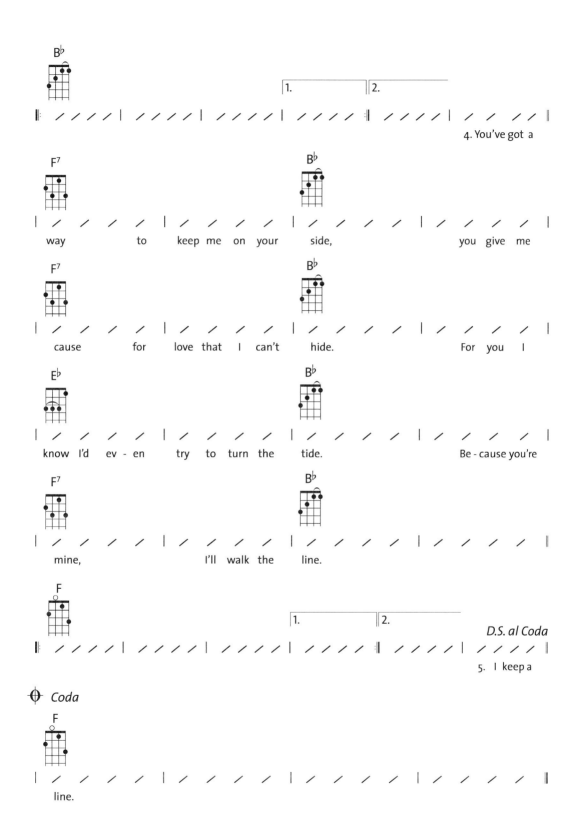

4. You've got a

way   to   keep me on your   side,   you give me

cause   for   love that I can't   hide.   For   you   I

know I'd   ev - en   try   to turn the   tide.   Be - cause you're

mine,   I'll walk the   line.

D.S. al Coda

5. I keep a

Coda

line.

it's a long way to tipperary

Words & Music by Jack Judge & Harry Williams

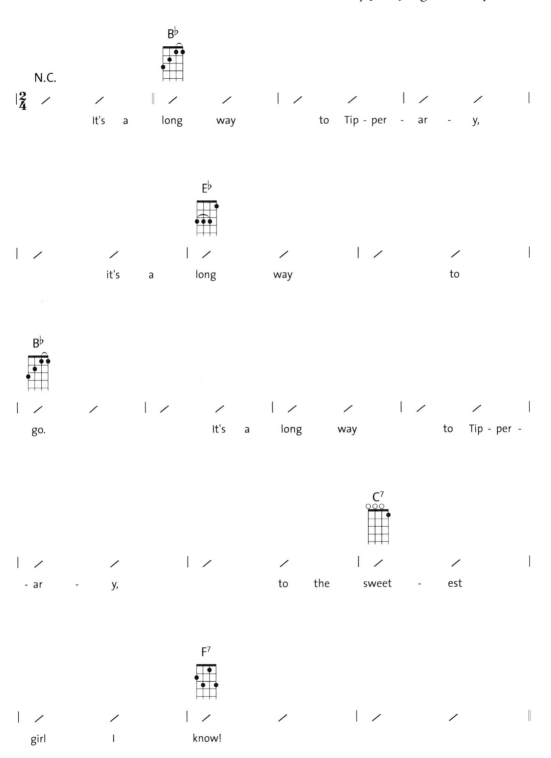

© Copyright 1912 B. Feldman & Company Limited.
All Rights Reserved. International Copyright Secured.

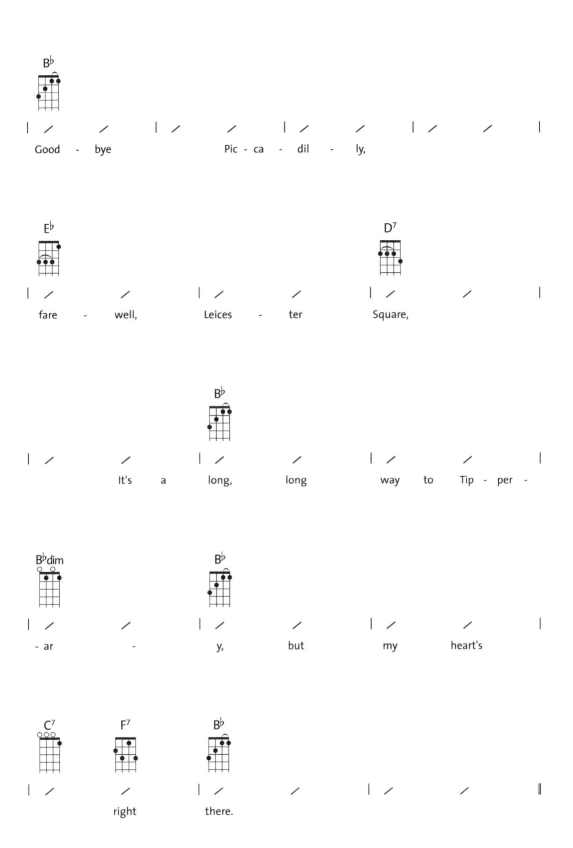

knockin' on heaven's door

Words & Music by Bob Dylan

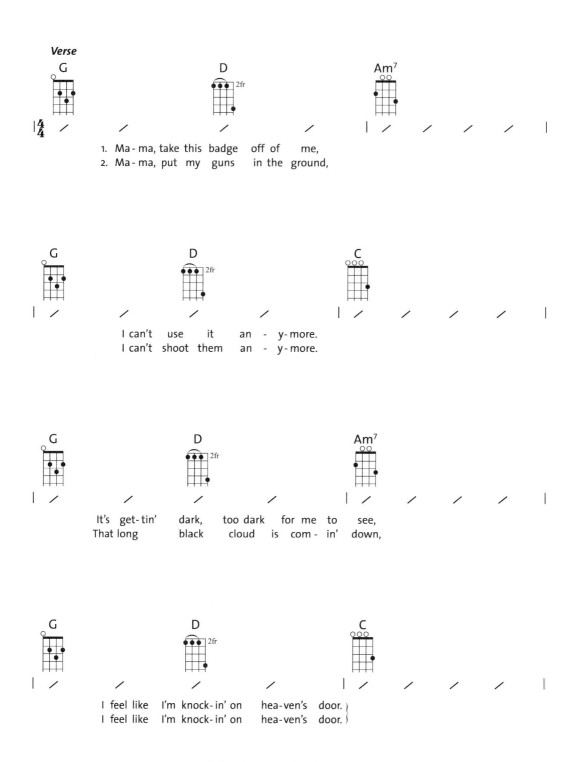

Verse

G   D   Am⁷

1. Ma - ma, take this badge off of me,
2. Ma - ma, put my guns in the ground,

G   D   C

I can't use it an - y - more.
I can't shoot them an - y - more.

G   D   Am⁷

It's get - tin' dark, too dark for me to see,
That long black cloud is com - in' down,

G   D   C

I feel like I'm knock - in' on hea - ven's door.
I feel like I'm knock - in' on hea - ven's door.

© Copyright 1973, 1974 Ram's Horn Music.
All Rights Reserved. International Copyright Secured.

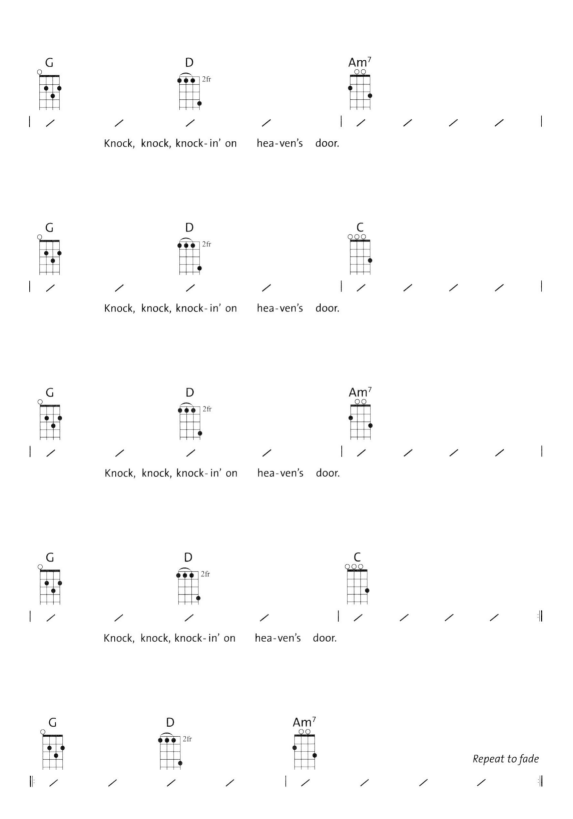

Knock, knock, knock-in' on hea-ven's door.

Knock, knock, knock-in' on hea-ven's door.

Knock, knock, knock-in' on hea-ven's door.

Knock, knock, knock-in' on hea-ven's door.

Repeat to fade

let her go

Words & Music by Michael Rosenberg

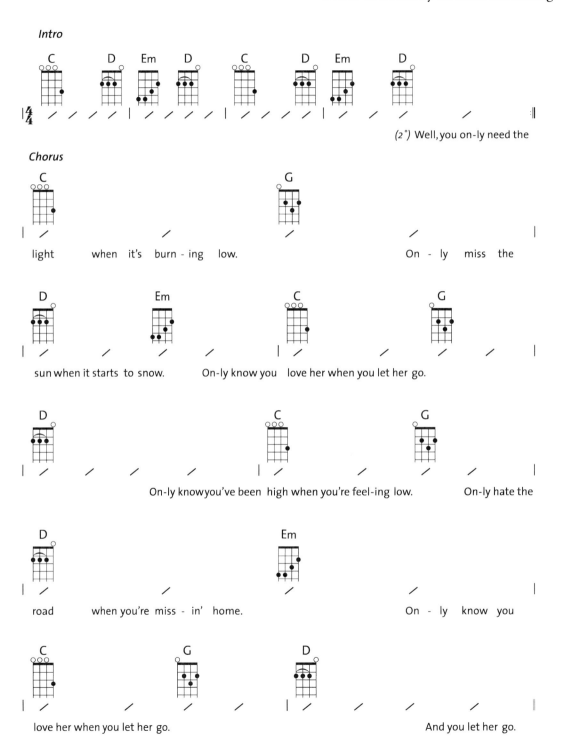

Intro

C   D   Em   D   C   D   Em   D

(2°) Well, you on-ly need the

Chorus

C   G

light   when it's burn - ing low.   On - ly miss the

D   Em   C   G

sun when it starts to snow.   On-ly know you   love her when you let her go.

D   C   G

On-ly know you've been high when you're feel-ing low.   On-ly hate the

D   Em

road   when you're miss - in' home.   On - ly know you

C   G   D

love her when you let her go.   And you let her go.

© Copyright 2012 Sony/ATV Music Publishing.
All Rights Reserved. International Copyright Secured.

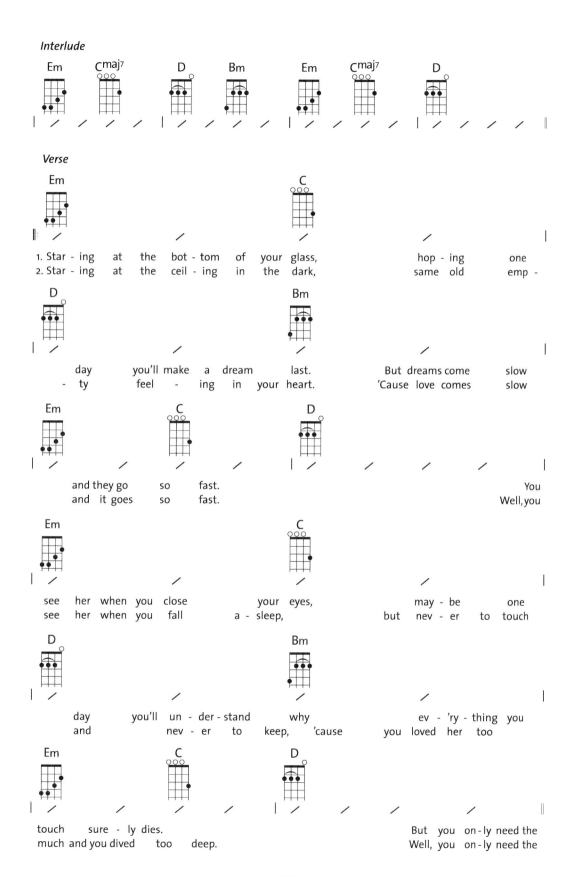

Interlude

Em Cmaj7 D Bm Em Cmaj7 D

Verse

Em   C

1. Star - ing   at   the   bot - tom   of   your glass,   hop - ing   one
2. Star - ing   at   the   ceil - ing   in   the   dark,   same   old   emp -

D   Bm

day   you'll make   a   dream   last.   But dreams come   slow
- ty   feel -   ing   in   your heart.   'Cause love comes   slow

Em   C   D

and they go   so   fast.   You
and   it goes   so   fast.   Well, you

Em   C

see   her when   you   close   your eyes,   may - be   one
see   her when   you   fall   a - sleep,   but   nev - er   to   touch

D   Bm

day   you'll   un - der - stand   why   ev - 'ry - thing you
and   nev - er   to   keep,   'cause   you   loved   her   too

Em   C   D

touch   sure - ly dies.   But   you on - ly need the
much   and you dived   too   deep.   Well, you   on - ly need the

29

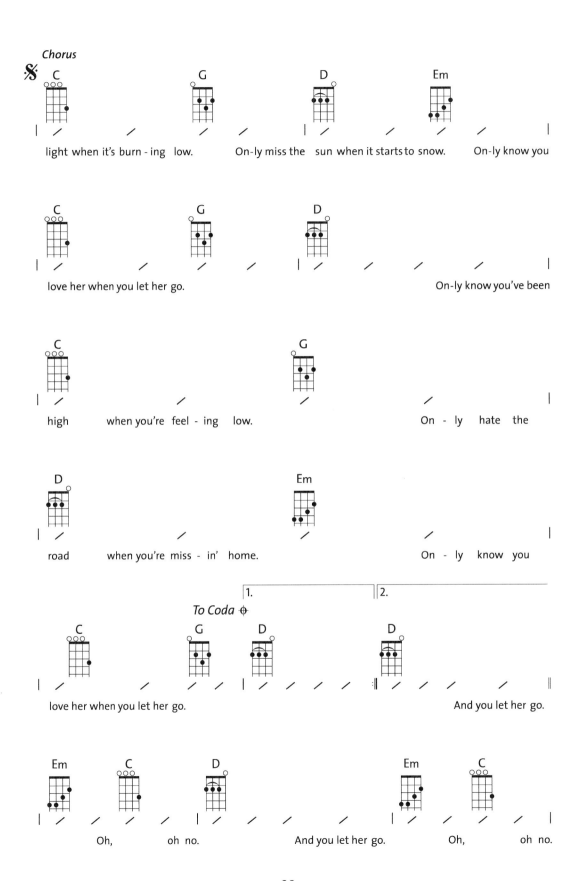

light when it's burn-ing low. On-ly miss the sun when it starts to snow. On-ly know you

love her when you let her go. On-ly know you've been

high when you're feel-ing low. On-ly hate the

road when you're miss-in' home. On-ly know you

To Coda

1.
love her when you let her go.

2.
And you let her go.

Oh, oh no. And you let her go. Oh, oh no.

30

love will tear us apart

Words & Music by Ian Curtis, Peter Hook, Bernard Sumner & Stephen Morris

Intro

Em⁷   D   Bm   A⁵

Em⁷   D   Bm   A⁵

1. When

Verse

Em⁷   D   Bm

(1.) rou - tine   bites   hard   and   am - bi - tions   are   low,
(2.) bed-room   so   cold,   turned a - way   on   your   side?
(3.) cry   out in your sleep,   all   my   fail-ings   ex -   posed?

A⁵   Em⁷   D

and re - sent - ment rides   high,   but e -
Is   my   tim - ing   that   flawed,   our re -
There's a   taste   in   my   mouth,   as des-per -

Bm   A⁵   Em⁷

- mo - tions   won't   grow,   and we're chan - ging our   ways,
- spect run   so   dry?   Yet there's still   this ap - peal
- a - tion   takes   hold.   Just that some - thing so   good,

© Copyright 1980 Universal Music Publishing Limited.
All Rights Reserved. International Copyright Secured.

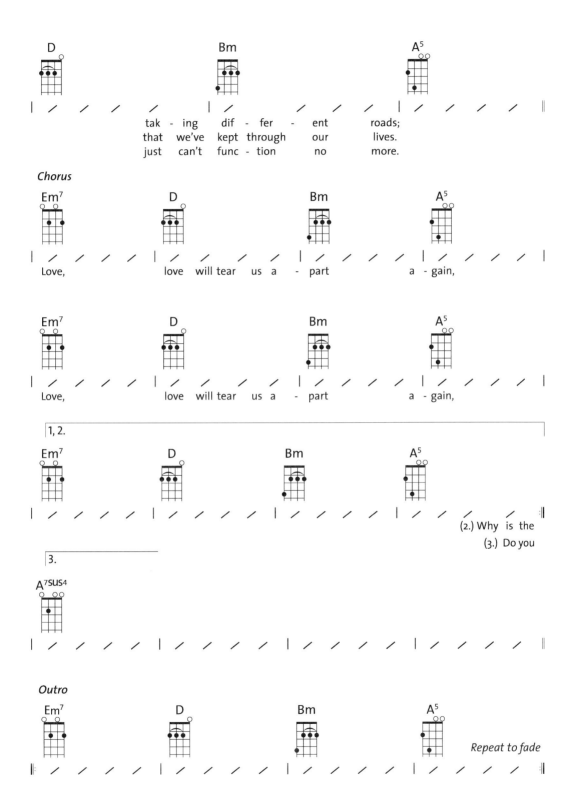

D   **Bm**   **A⁵**

tak - ing   dif - fer - ent   roads;
that   we've   kept   through   our   lives.
just   can't   func - tion   no   more.

Chorus

Em⁷   **D**   **Bm**   **A⁵**

Love,   love   will   tear   us   a - part   a - gain,

Em⁷   **D**   **Bm**   **A⁵**

Love,   love   will   tear   us   a - part   a - gain,

1, 2.

Em⁷   **D**   **Bm**   **A⁵**

(2.) Why is the
(3.) Do you

3.

A⁷SUS4

Outro

Em⁷   **D**   **Bm**   **A⁵**

Repeat to fade

33

norwegian wood
(this bird has flown)

Words & Music by John Lennon & Paul McCartney

Intro

Instrumental

Verse

1. I once had a girl, or should I say, she once had me.

She showed me her room, is-n't it good, Nor-we-gian Wood? She

Chorus

(1.) asked me to stay and she told me to sit an-y-where. So
(2.) told me she worked in the morn-ing and start-ed to laugh; I

I looked a-round and I no-ticed there was-n't a chair.
told her I did-n't and crawled off the sleep in the bath.

© Copyright 1965 Sony/ATV Music Publishing.
All Rights Reserved. International Copyright Secured.

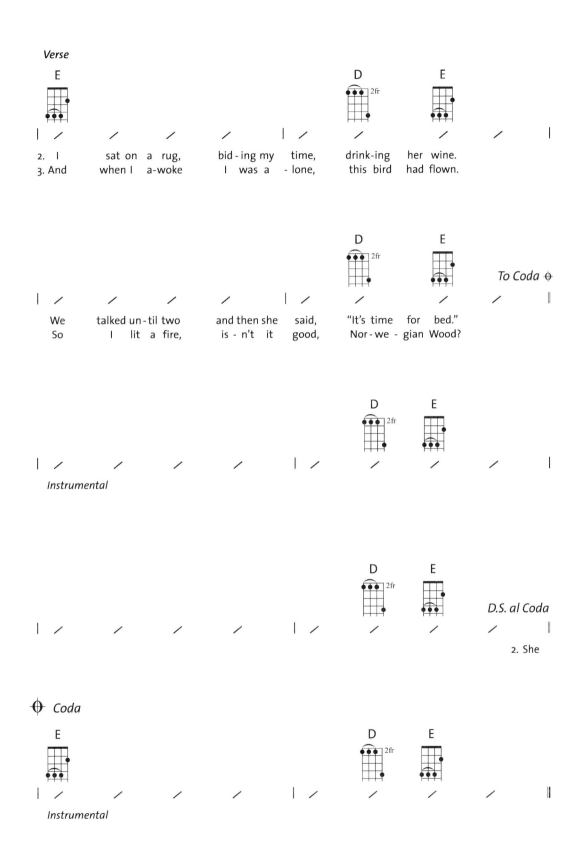

Verse

E   D   E

2. I   sat on a rug,   bid-ing my time,   drink-ing her wine.
3. And   when I a-woke   I was a - lone,   this bird had flown.

D   E   *To Coda* ⊕

We   talked un-til two   and then she said,   "It's time for bed."
So   I lit a fire,   is-n't it good,   Nor-we-gian Wood?

D   E

Instrumental

D   E   *D.S. al Coda*

2. She

⊕ *Coda*

E   D   E

Instrumental

on top of old smoky

Traditional

F

$\frac{3}{4}$ ╱ ‖ ╱ ╱ ╱ │ ╱ ╱ ╱ │ ╱ ╱ ╱ │ ╱ ╱ ╱ │

1. On   top of   Old   Smo -   ky,   all
2. Well a - court-ing's a   plea -   sure,   and
3. A   thief he will   rob   you   and
4. And the grave will de - cay   you   and

(Verses 5-8 see block lyrics)

C

│ ╱ ╱ ╱ │ ╱ ╱ ╱ │ ╱ ╱ ╱ │ ╱ ╱ ╱ │

co - vered with   snow,   I
part - ing is   grief.   But a
take   all   you   have,   but a
turn you to   dust.   And

G⁷

│ ╱ ╱ ╱ │ ╱ ╱ ╱ │ ╱ ╱ ╱ │ ╱ ╱ ╱ │

lost my   true   lo -   ver,   by a
false - heart - ed lo -   ver,   is
false - heart - ed lo -   ver   will send
where is   the   young   man   a

© Copyright 2013 Dorsey Brothers Music Limited.
All Rights Reserved. International Copyright Secured.

C

| ╱ ╱ ╱ | ╱ ╱ ╱ | ╱ ╱ ╱ | ╱ ╱ ╱ ‖

court - in'   too   slow.
worse   than   a   thief.
you   to   your   grave.
poor   girl   can   trust?

5. They'll hug you and kiss you,
   And tell you more lies
   Than the crossties on the railroad,
   Or the stars in the skies.

6. They'll tell you they love you,
   Just to give your heart ease.
   But the minute your back's turned,
   They'll court whom they please.

7. So come all you young maidens
   And listen to me.
   Never place your affection
   On a green willow tree.

8. For the leaves they will wither
   And the roots they will die,
   And your true love will leave you
   And you'll never know why.

raindrops keep fallin' on my head

Words by Hal David
Music by Burt Bacharach

© Copyright 1969 WB Music Corporation/New Hidden Valley Music Company/Casa David Music Incorporated.
Warner/Chappell Music North America Limited/Warner/Chappell Music/Universal/MCA Music Limited.
All Rights Reserved. International Copyright Secured.

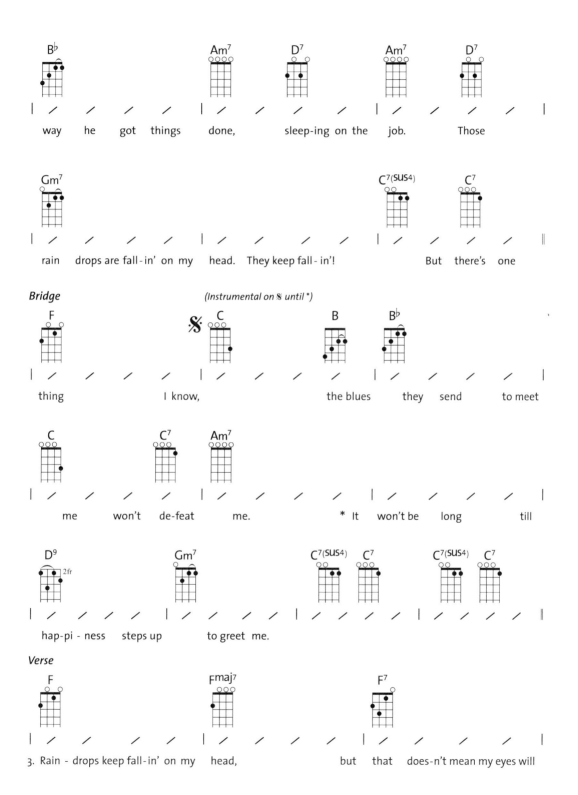

way he got things done, sleep-ing on the job. Those

rain drops are fall-in' on my head. They keep fall-in'! But there's one

Bridge *(Instrumental on 𝄋 until *)*

thing I know, the blues they send to meet

me won't de-feat me. * It won't be long till

hap-pi - ness steps up to greet me.

Verse

3. Rain - drops keep fall-in' on my head, but that does-n't mean my eyes will

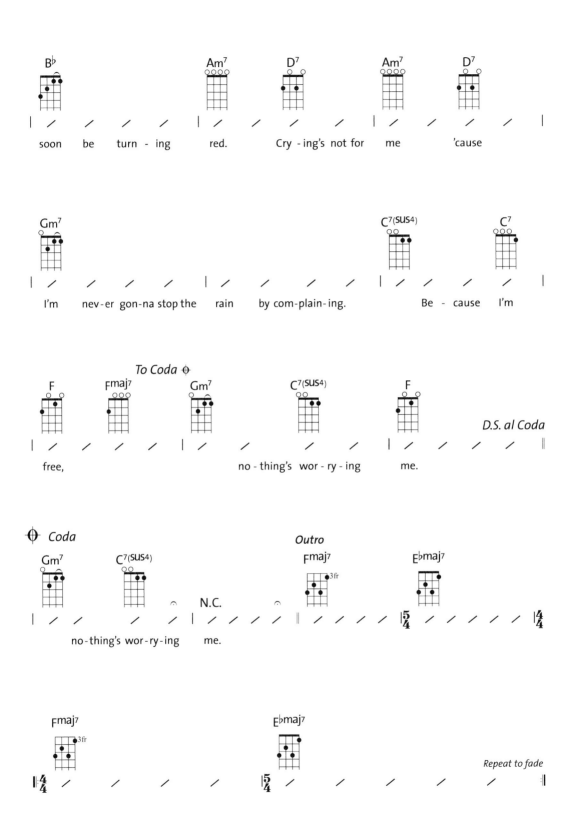

set fire to the rain

Words & Music by Fraser Smith & Adele Adkins

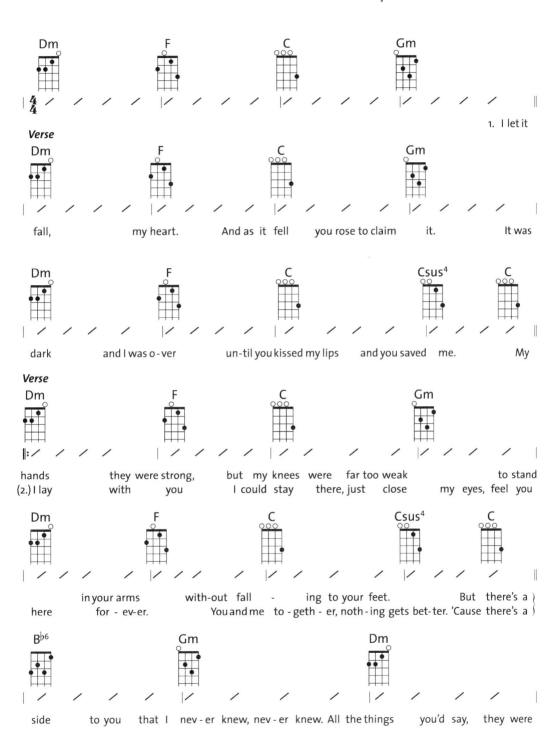

1. I let it fall, my heart. And as it fell you rose to claim it. It was dark and I was o-ver un-til you kissed my lips and you saved me. My

Verse

hands they were strong,
(2.) I lay with you

but my knees were far too weak to stand
I could stay there, just close my eyes, feel you

in your arms with-out fall - ing to your feet. But there's a
here for - ev-er. You and me to - geth - er, noth-ing gets bet-ter. 'Cause there's a

side to you that I nev - er knew, nev - er knew. All the things you'd say, they were

© Copyright 2010 Melted Stone Publishing Ltd.
Chrysalis Music Limited/Universal Music Publishing Limited.
All Rights Reserved. International Copyright Secured.

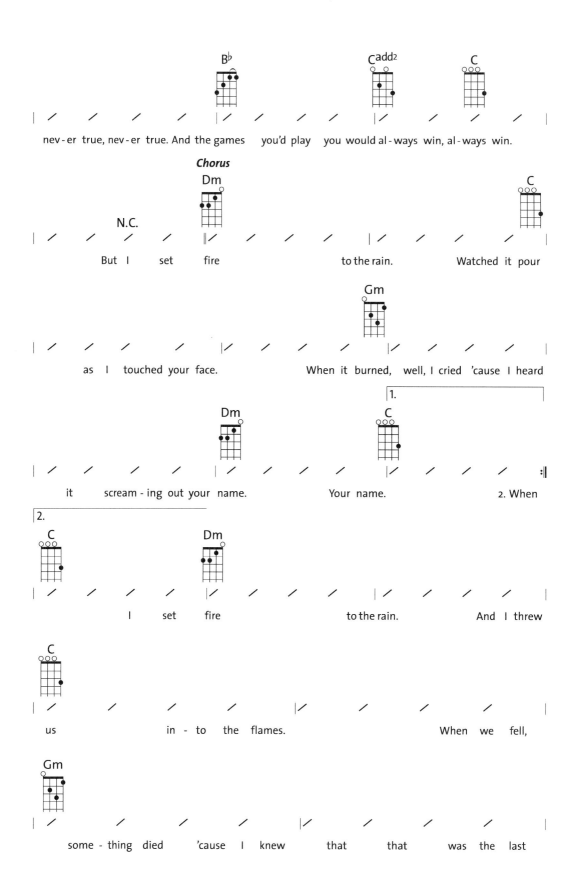

B♭

Cadd2

C

| / / / / | / / / / | / / / / |

nev - er true, nev - er true. And the games   you'd play   you would al - ways win, al - ways win.

Chorus

Dm

C

N.C.

| / / / / |‖ / / / / | / / / / |

But I   set   fire   to the rain.   Watched it pour

Gm

| / / / / | / / / / | / / / / |

as   I   touched your face.   When it burned,   well, I cried 'cause I heard

1.

Dm

C

| / / / / | / / / / | / / / / :‖

it   scream - ing out your   name.   Your name.   2. When

2.

C

Dm

| / / / / | / / / | / / / |

I   set   fire   to the rain.   And I threw

C

| / / / / | / / / |

us   in - to   the   flames.   When we   fell,

Gm

| / / / / | / / / |

some - thing died   'cause   I   knew   that   that   was   the   last

42

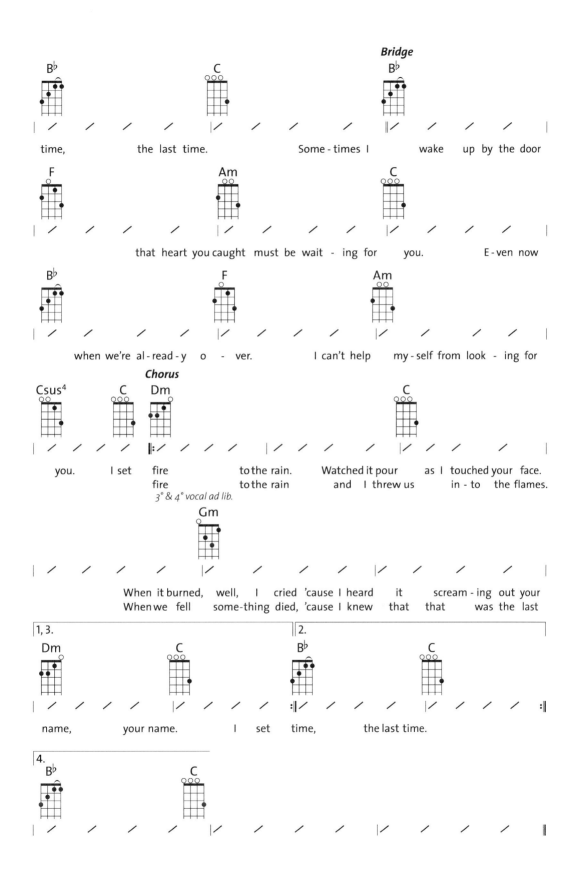

Bridge

B♭   C   B♭

| / / / / | / / / | | / / / |

time,   the last time.   Some - times I   wake   up by the door

F   Am   C

| / / / / | / / / / | / / / |

that heart you caught must be wait - ing for   you.   E - ven now

B♭   F   Am

| / / / / | / / / / | / / / |

when we're al - read - y   o - ver.   I can't help   my - self from look - ing for

Chorus

Csus⁴   C   Dm   C

| / / / / |: / / / | / / / | / / / |

you.   I set   fire   to the rain.   Watched it pour   as I touched your face.
               fire   to the rain   and I threw us   in - to the flames.

3° & 4° vocal ad lib.

Gm

| / / / / | / / / | / / / |

When it burned,   well,   I   cried 'cause I heard   it   scream - ing out your
When we fell   some - thing died, 'cause I knew   that   that   was the last

| 1, 3. | 2.

Dm   C   B♭   C

| / / / / | / / / / :|| / / / | / / / / :|

name,   your name.   I   set   time,   the last time.

| 4.

B♭   C

| / / / / | / / / / | / / / ‖

somewhere only we know

Words & Music by Richard Hughes, Tim Rice-Oxley & Tom Chaplin

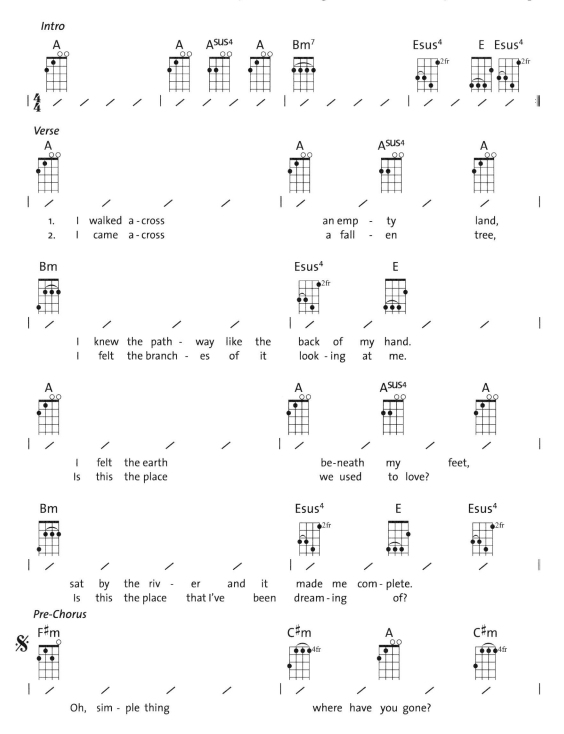

© Copyright 2004 BMG Music Publishing Limited.
Universal Music Publishing MGB Limited.
All Rights Reserved. International Copyright Secured.

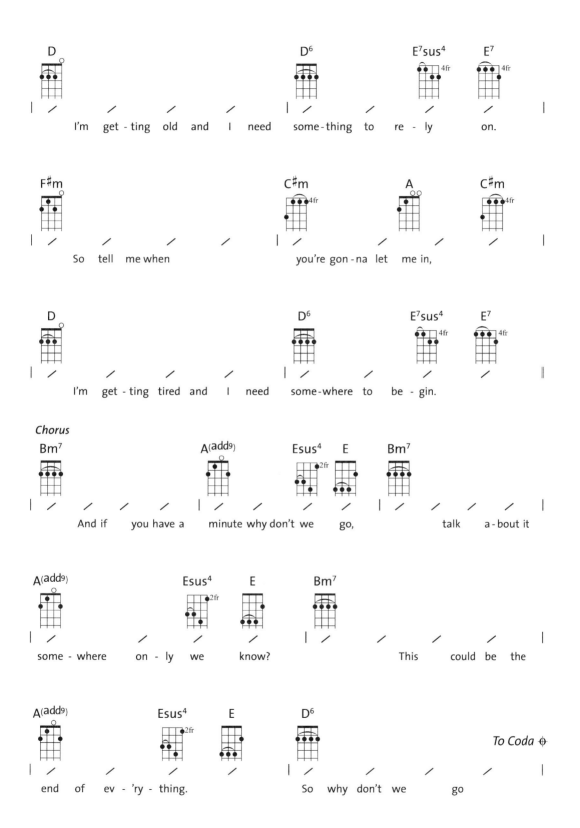

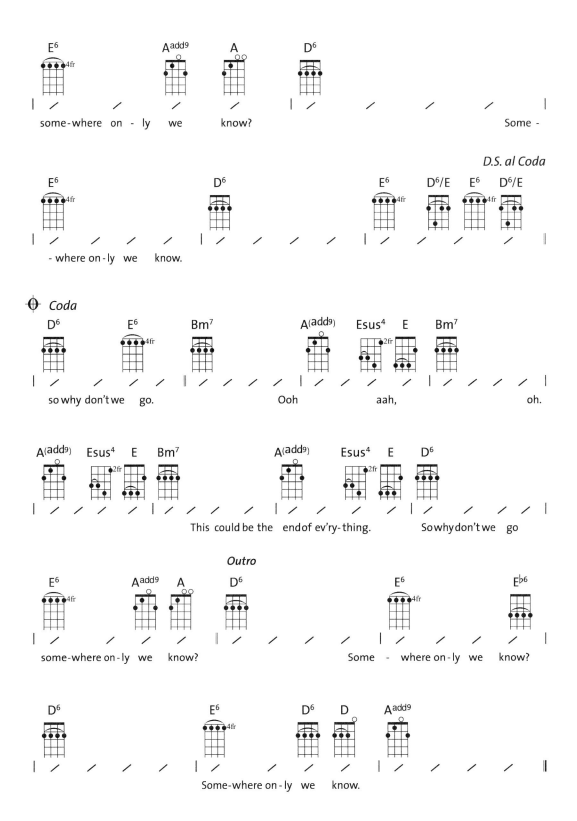

some-where on - ly we know? Some -

D.S. al Coda

- where on - ly we know.

Coda

so why don't we go. Ooh aah, oh.

This could be the end of ev'ry-thing. So why don't we go

Outro

some-where on - ly we know? Some - where on - ly we know?

Some-where on - ly we know.

46

sweet caroline

Words & Music by Neil Diamond

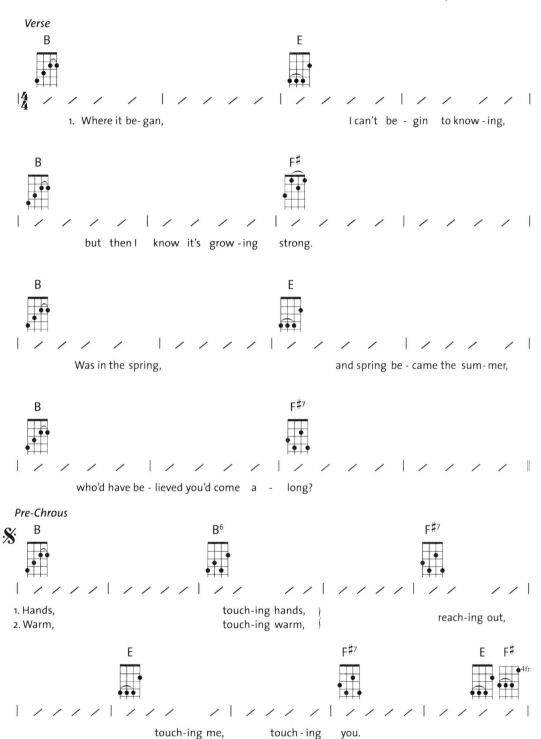

© Copyright 1969 Stonebridge Music Incorporated.
Sony/ATV Music Publishing.
All Rights Reserved. International Copyright Secured.

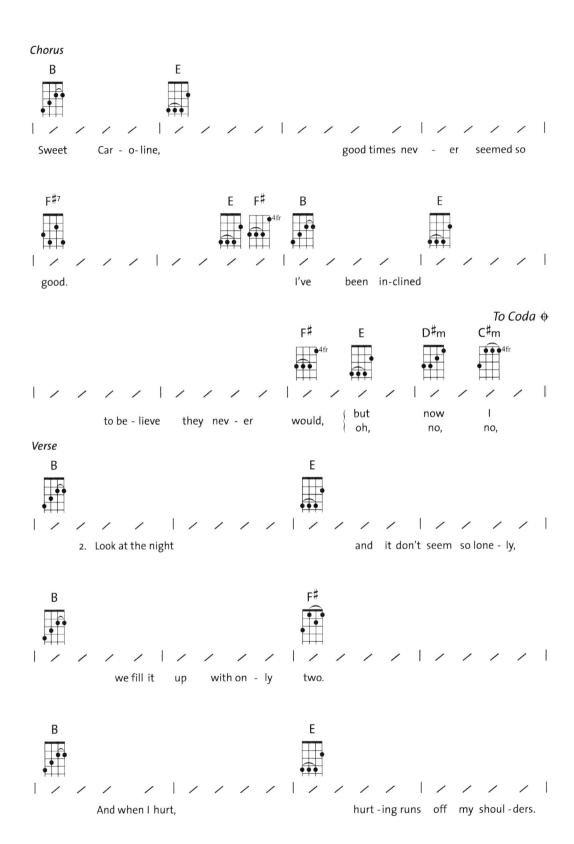

Chorus

B   E

Sweet   Car - o- line,   good times nev - er   seemed so

F#7   E F# B   E

good.   I've   been in-clined

To Coda

F#   E   D#m C#m

to be - lieve   they nev - er   would, { but   now   I
                                           oh,   no,   no,

Verse

B   E

2. Look at the night   and it don't seem so lone - ly,

B   F#

we fill it   up   with on - ly   two.

B   E

And when I hurt,   hurt -ing runs off my shoul -ders.

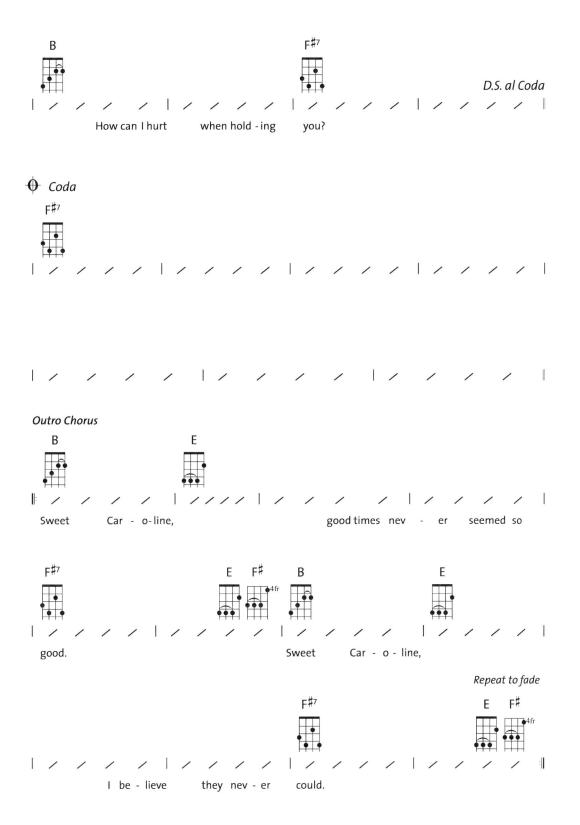

B   F#7   *D.S. al Coda*

How can I hurt   when hold - ing   you?

Coda

F#7

Outro Chorus

B   E

Sweet   Car - o-line,   good times nev - er   seemed so

F#7   E   F#   B   E

good.   Sweet   Car - o - line,

Repeat to fade

F#7   E   F#

I be - lieve   they nev - er   could.

stand by me

Words & Music by Ben E. King, Jerry Leiber & Mike Stoller

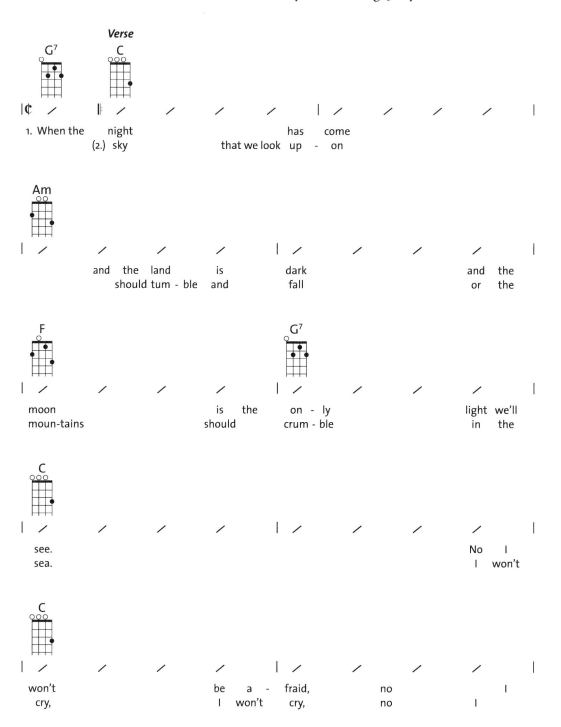

1. When the   night   has   come
   (2.) sky   that we look up - on

and   the   land   is   dark   and   the
should tum - ble   and   fall   or   the

moon   is   the   on - ly   light we'll
moun-tains   should   crum - ble   in   the

see.   No   I
sea.   I   won't

won't   be   a - fraid,   no   I
cry,   I   won't   cry,   no   I

© Copyright 1961 Sony/ATV Tunes LLC, USA.
Administered by Hal Leonard.
All Rights Reserved. International Copyright Secured.

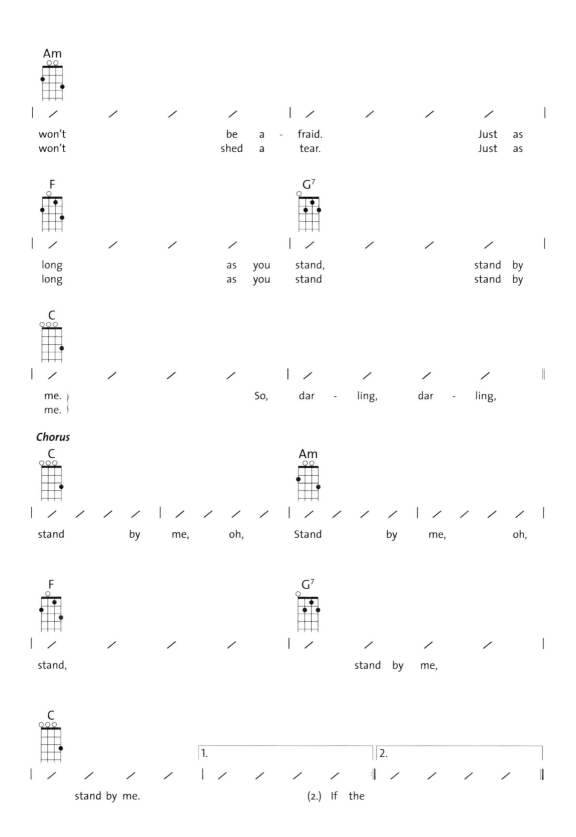

Am

won't   be   a - fraid.   Just   as
won't   shed   a   tear.   Just   as

F   **G⁷**

long   as   you   stand,   stand   by
long   as   you   stand   stand   by

C

me. ⎱
me. ⎰   So,   dar - ling,   dar - ling,

Chorus

C   **Am**

stand   by   me,   oh,   Stand   by   me,   oh,

F   **G⁷**

stand,   stand   by   me,

C

             1.   2.

stand by me.   (2.) If   the

will the circle be unbroken

Traditional

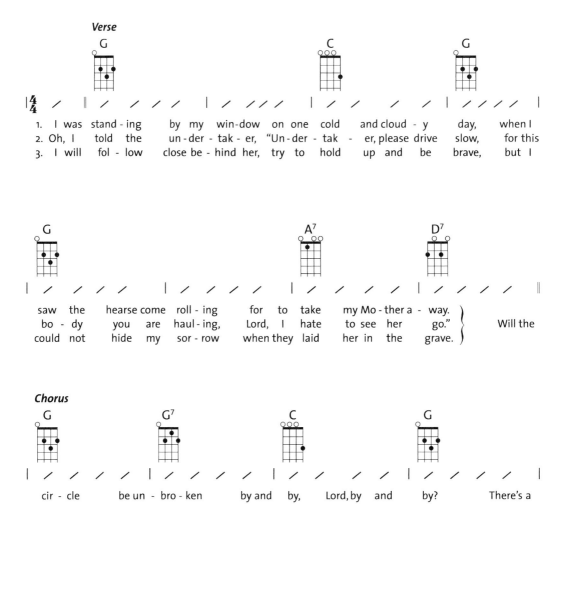

Verse

G | C | G |

1. I was stand-ing by my win-dow on one cold and cloud-y day, when I
2. Oh, I told the un-der-tak-er, "Un-der-tak-er, please drive slow, for this
3. I will fol-low close be-hind her, try to hold up and be brave, but I

G | A7 | D7 |

saw the hearse come roll-ing for to take my Mo-ther a-way.
bo-dy you are haul-ing, Lord, I hate to see her go." } Will the
could not hide my sor-row when they laid her in the grave.

Chorus

G | G7 | C | G |

cir-cle be un-bro-ken by and by, Lord, by and by? There's a

C | G | D7 | G |

bet-ter home a-wait-ing in the sky, in the sky.

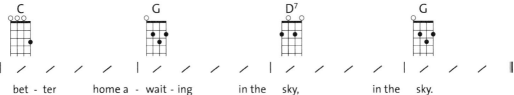

© Copyright 2013 Dorsey Brothers Music Limited.
All Rights Reserved. International Copyright Secured.

the winner takes it all

Words & Music by Benny Andersson & Björn Ulvaeus

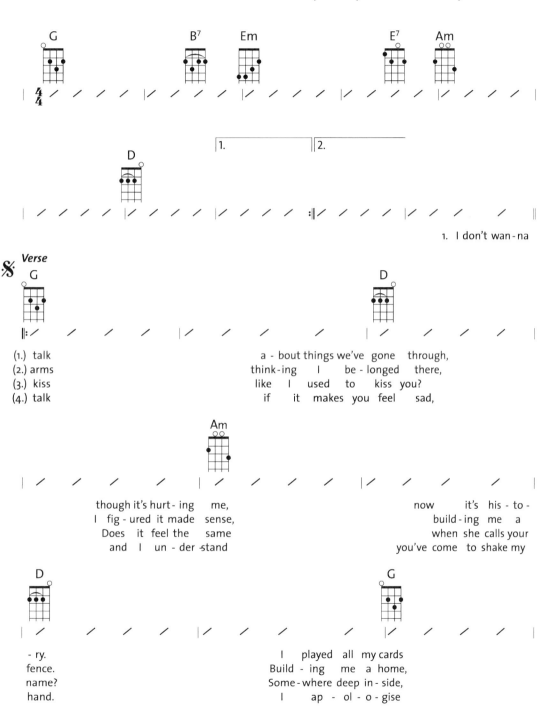

1. I don't wan-na

Verse

(1.) talk   a - bout things we've gone through,
(2.) arms   think-ing I be-longed there,
(3.) kiss   like I used to kiss you?
(4.) talk   if it makes you feel sad,

though it's hurt-ing me,   now it's his-to-
I fig-ured it made sense,   build-ing me a
Does it feel the same   when she calls your
and I un-der-stand   you've come to shake my

- ry.   I played all my cards
fence.   Build - ing me a home,
name?   Some-where deep in-side,
hand.   I ap - ol - o - gise

© Copyright 1980 Union Songs AB, Sweden.
Bocu Music Limited for Great Britain and the Republic of Ireland.
All Rights Reserved. International Copyright Secured.

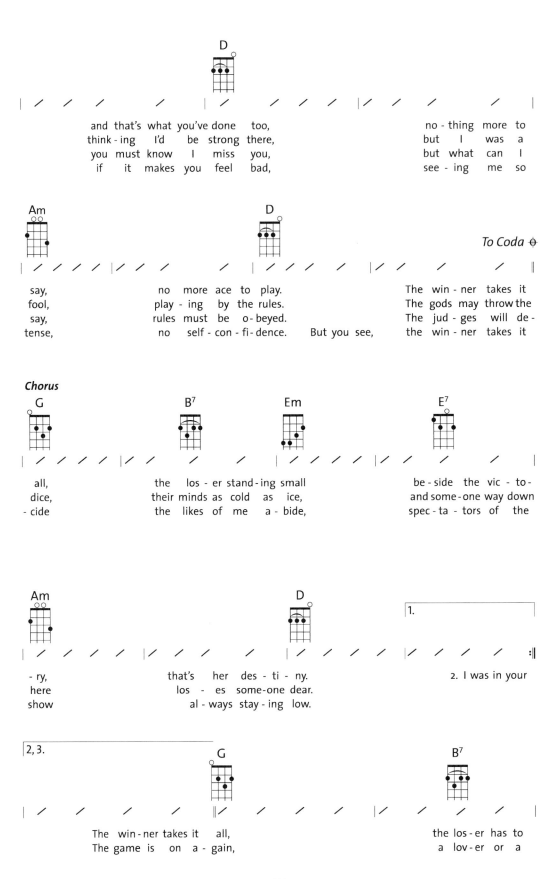

D

| ╱ ╱ ╱ ╱ | ╱ ╱ ╱ ╱ | ╱ ╱ ╱ ╱ |

and that's what you've done   too,
think - ing   I'd   be strong there,
you must know   I   miss   you,
if   it   makes you   feel   bad,

no - thing more to
but   I   was   a
but what   can   I
see - ing   me   so

Am   **D**

To Coda ⊕

| ╱ ╱ ╱ ╱ | ╱ ╱ ╱ ╱ | ╱ ╱ ╱ ╱ | ╱ ╱ ╱ ╱ ‖

say,   no   more ace to   play.
fool,   play - ing   by the rules.
say,   rules must be   o - beyed.
tense,   no   self - con - fi - dence.   But you see,

The   win - ner   takes it
The   gods may throw the
The   jud - ges   will de -
the   win - ner   takes it

Chorus

G   **B⁷**   **Em**   **E⁷**

| ╱ ╱ ╱ ╱ | ╱ ╱ ╱ ╱ | ╱ ╱ ╱ ╱ | ╱ ╱ ╱ ╱ |

all,   the   los - er stand - ing small
dice,   their minds as cold   as   ice,
- cide   the   likes of me   a - bide,

be - side   the vic - to -
and some - one way down
spec - ta - tors of   the

Am   **D**   1.

| ╱ ╱ ╱ ╱ | ╱ ╱ ╱ ╱ | ╱ ╱ ╱ ╱ | ╱ ╱ ╱ ╱ ‖

- ry,   that's   her   des - ti - ny.
here   los - es   some - one dear.
show   al - ways stay - ing   low.

2. I was in your

2, 3.   **G**   **B⁷**

| ╱ ╱ ╱ ╱ ‖ ╱ ╱ ╱ ╱ | ╱ ╱ ╱ ╱ |

The   win - ner takes it   all,
The   game is   on   a - gain,

the los - er has to
a   lov - er or a

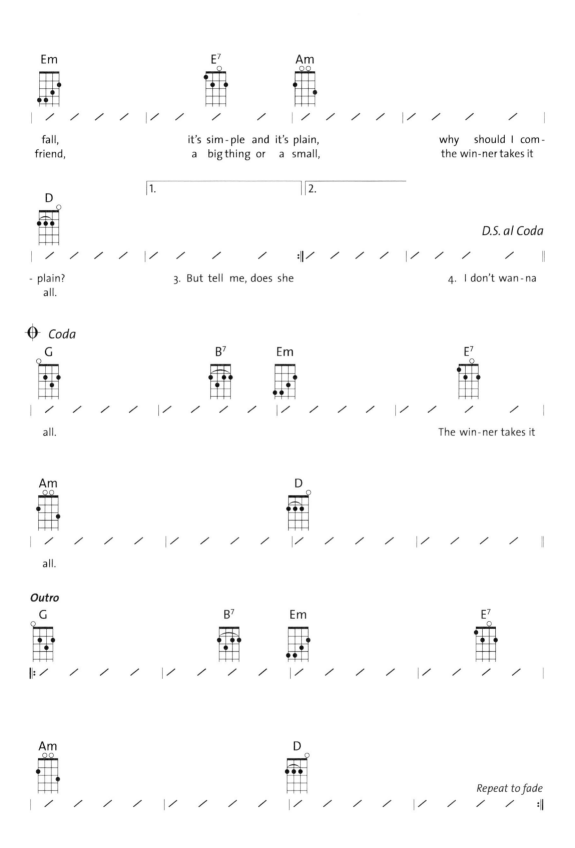

Em

E⁷ **Am**

| / / / / | / / / / | / / / / | / / / / |

fall,   it's sim-ple and it's plain,   why should I com-
friend,   a big thing or a small,   the win-ner takes it

     1.   2.

D

D.S. al Coda

| / / / / | / / / / :|| / / / / | / / / / ||

- plain? 3. But tell me, does she   4. I don't wan-na
all.

⊕ Coda

G   **B⁷** **Em**   **E⁷**

| / / / / | / / / / | / / / / | / / / / |

all.   The win-ner takes it

Am   **D**

| / / / / | / / / / | / / / / | / / / / ||

all.

Outro

G   **B⁷** **Em**   **E⁷**

||: / / / / | / / / / | / / / / | / / / / |

Am   **D**

Repeat to fade

| / / / / | / / / / | / / / / | / / / / :||

If you enjoyed this book you may be interested in these

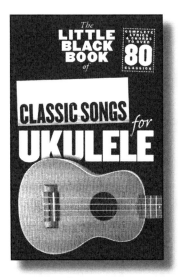

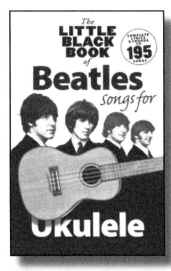

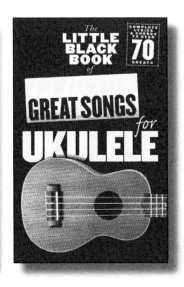

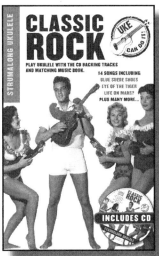

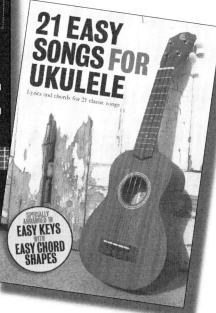

Available from all good music shops.
In case of difficulty please contact
Hal Leonard Europe Limited
Newmarket Road Bury St Edmunds,
Suffolk, IP33 3YB, UK.

www.halleonard.com